CHAMPIONS OF FREEDOM

The Ludwig von Mises Lecture Series

CHAMPIONS OF FREEDOM
Volume 16

THE FREE MARKET AND THE BLACK COMMUNITY

Ronald L. Trowbridge, Executive Editor
Lissa Roche, General Editor

Hillsdale College Press
Hillsdale, Michigan 49242

Hillsdale College Press

Books by the Hillsdale College Press include the *Champions of Freedom* series on economics; *The Christian Vision* series; and other works.

CHAMPIONS OF FREEDOM:
THE FREE MARKET AND THE BLACK COMMUNITY
© 1990 by Hillsdale College Press
Hillsdale, Michigan 49242

First Printing 1990
Library of Congress Catalog Card Number 89-085912
ISBN 0-916308-85-5

Contents

Preface

Ludwig von Mises, who died in 1973 at the age of 92, was one of our century's most prominent defenders of human liberty and a dedicated opponent of governmental intervention in the economy. Through his scholarship, writing and teaching, Mises argued powerfully for individual freedom, private property, free markets, and limited government. His theory of economics was based on the supremacy of the individual and the rational, purposeful day-to-day decisions of the individual that constitute the market. His description of the market as a process, set against a background of fluctuating conditions, was a decisive departure from other contemporary economists' "models" of mathematical rigidity.

In nineteen books, including his famous *Human Action* and *The Theory of Money and Credit,* hundreds of articles and countless lectures, Dr. von Mises successfully proved that a free society cannot exist without a free economy. However, he wrote his books at a time when the dominant thinking in economics ran counter to his own theories. On this subject, in his own words, he said:

> Occasionally, I entertained the hope that my writings would bear practical fruit and show the

way for policy. Constantly I have been looking for evidence of a change in ideology. But I have never allowed myself to be deceived. I have come to realize that my theories explain the degeneration of a great civilization; they do not prevent it. I set out to be a reformer, but only became the historian of decline.

When the history of twentieth-century thought is written, Ludwig von Mises will, in all probability, be recognized as the greatest economist of our age. This may be wishful thinking, but I suspect not. I believe the truth always triumphs. It is always recognized, if only, as the economist is so fond of saying, in the long run. Without a doubt, when socialism is dead, when Marx is finally laid to rest, and when Keynesian economics is finally fully discredited, still Mises will live on.

George Roche
President
Hillsdale College

Foreword

Before the emergence of liberal capitalism in the late eighteenth and early nineteenth centuries every one in society "knew their place." Class distinction and caste position determined the social ranking of practically every member of society from birth to death. To try to rise above your class and social position was considered pretentious, and to associate too closely with those in lower classes was considered demeaning. The precapitalist order also guaranteed some in the society great wealth and privilege, while others were only assured extreme poverty and bondage.

Liberal capitalism brought an end to the society of status. In its place arose the society of freedom. In *The Wealth of Nations,* Adam Smith proposed a "system of natural liberty," in which "Every man, as long as he does not violate the laws of justice, is left perfectly free to pursue his own interest his own way, and to bring his industry and capital into competition with those of any other man, or order of men."

Here was truly a revolution of liberation. The system of natural liberty required each individual to be recognized as possessing rights to life, liberty, and property, and to be sovereign in pursuing "his own interests his own way" as long as he respected the same rights of all other men to do the same. With the development of liberal capitalism, "class" and "class distinctions" were reduced to matters of social graces, etiquette and manners, and aesthetic tastes. Which "class" an individual belonged to in this new sense was now determined, to a great extent, by personal choice and conduct.

Nor was wealth and access to wealth any longer a matter of birth or political privilege. Under the new system of natural liberty every individual was free "to bring his industry and his capital into competition with those of any other man." As the nineteenth century progressed, the legal and political barriers that had stood in the way of individuals pursuing any trade, profession, or occupation of their own choice came tumbling down. The marketplace increasingly became an arena of open, free, and unlimited competition that welcomed all who wished to try.

In the new world of free market capitalism, the avenue to wealth and prosperity was more and more available to all. How wealthy a man became was determined by one criterion: how well an individual could adjust his behavior in the market to satisfying the wants and desires of the consuming public. A capitalist economy is distinguishable by two institutions: private property in the means of production, and voluntary exchange. Individuals are permitted to own both capital and land, and use them within a wide range of discretion as they see fit. But how that private property is used is heavily influenced by the requirement that all transactions and exchanges be mutually agreed upon by the traders in the market.

Every individual who wishes to be a consumer of what others have for sale can only acquire the necessary financial means to do so if he first offers a product or service to others that they are willing to buy at an agreed upon price. In other words, each individual as a producer must direct his actions (with his labor, land, and capital) to satisfying the consumer demands of others in the society. Only by being successful in this endeavor does he acquire the income that enables him to be a consumer himself. Each individual's wealth and buying power in the market, therefore, is a function of how well he has served his fellow men as a producer.

The free market economy, as a result, tends to judge each person by their ability to "deliver the desired goods" better than some other individual who is competing against him for the consumers' business. In the free market work place, racial, ethnic, religious, or sexual prejudice now impose a heavy cost. The businessman who allows such biases to guide his hiring and contracting decisions runs the risk of losing or passing up the better worker or contractor whose greater productive ability or efficiency could have meant the marketing of a better or less expensive product that would have attracted more consumers to what he has for sale. On the other hand, the employer who tends to disregard race, ethnicity, religion, or sex in his hiring practices, therefore, can gain the competitive edge and potentially increase his profits and income.

But in the historical development of the market economy, not all people were recognized as free and possessing equal rights. When the nineteenth century began, slavery still existed as an institution through most of the Western world. But the logic of Adam Smith's system of natural liberty meant that this could not last. The classical economists argued that free labor was inherently more productive than slave labor, and that the maintenance of slavery, from the economic point of view, resulted in a materially poorer society; free men had incentives to work productively, and in an open, free labor market, competition would direct their production into those areas that would best satisfy consumer demand.

The logic of a system of natural liberty also lead political philosophers, intellectuals, and increasing numbers of the general public to question the morality of societies that existed half-free and half-slave. In England, the "Anti-Slavery League" was formed, millions of dollars were collected by voluntary donations, and thousands of slaves had their freedom bought for them. Finally, in the 1830s, Parliament abolished slavery in the British Empire. In the United States, slavery came to an end in the 1860s through a violent Civil War that cost the lives of more than 600,000. And in 1898, the Empress of

Brazil signed a document that peacefully ended black slavery in her country and, therefore, in the Western hemisphere.

But if liberal capitalism has historically meant political and economic liberation for the individual from the old regime of status and privilege, and if the market economy has tended to penalize racism and reward the judging of people as individuals, why, then, have large segments of the black community in America failed to enter the economic and social mainstream?

In fact, as economist Thomas Sowell and others have shown with a wealth of historical evidence, significant economic improvements had been and were being made up to about twenty-five years ago. And the black family was one of the most stable social units in the United States throughout most of this century. There was no reason to believe that the future would be any different. But as Charles Murray dramatically demonstrated in his book, *Losing Ground,* both the economic advancement and family stability of a large number in the American black community has been weakened, if not reversed, during the last quarter century. Why?

The answer, paradoxically, has been the welfare state and the interventionist state. The welfare and regulatory institutions created and designed with the intention of helping those at the bottom of the social and economic ladder have been the very institutions that have prevented those people from rising up from poverty. The rules and procedures for obtaining welfare assistance have weakened incentives for work; they have broken up family units and destroyed the home environment that is crucial for generational transmission of the personal and social values essential for individual achievement. Minimum wage laws and licensing procedures for starting and running small businesses have closed the door to millions who otherwise might have found job opportunities in the labor market or begun their way toward wealth through self-employment.

Indeed, the paternalistic state has created a new slavery in the form of dependency upon the government. Locked out of the market by regulations and employment laws, many blacks in the United States have had no recourse but to fall back on government welfarism for survival. And once in that state of dependency, they soon find that all the rules and incentives are tacitly designed to keep them there. Millions of black Americans have been reduced to a new bondage, subject to new masters in a vast governmental bureaucracy.

It also needs to be pointed out that the dilemma that confronts the black community under the existing welfare system is not due to any issue of race. Indeed, many on welfare are not black. The dilemma has been caused by the perverse incentives that the welfare state has erected over time. In the past, when similar welfare institutions have been put in place, similar results have followed. In 1871, one of the last of the great classical economists in England, Henry Fawcett, published a book entitled, *Pauperism: Its Causes and Remedies*. Pockets of severe poverty, he explained, existed in England at the very time of a growing and expanding British economy in which many in the society were obtaining rising standards of living that had never been known before. A primary culprit for this poverty amongst plenty, Fawcett argued, was the "Poor Laws," *i.e.*, the English welfare programs that had been in effect since Queen Elizabeth I. The incentives of the Poor Laws system and the consequences that followed from them were no different from what we have seen in America in our own times. In Fawcett's words of 1871:

> ... [M]en were virtually told that no amount of recklessness, self-indulgence, or improvidence would in the slightest degree affect their claim to be maintained at other people's expense. If they married when they had no reasonable chance of being able to maintain a family, they were treated as if they had performed a meritorious act, for the more children they had the greater was the amount of relief obtained. All the most evident teachings of common sense were completely set to nought.... An artificial stimulus was thus given to population.... Population was also fostered by a still more immoral stimulus. A woman obtained from the parish [the local agency for the distribution of welfare] a larger allowance for an illegitimate

than for a legitimate child. From one end of the kingdom to the other people were in fact told not only to marry with utter recklessness and let others bear the consequences, but it was also said, especially to the women of the country the greater is your immorality, the greater will be your pecuniary reward. Can it excite surprise that from such a system we have had handed down to us a vast inheritance of vice and poverty?

And Fawcett pointed out to his English readers that the welfare programs of his day had created dependency "by successive generations of the same family." He reported that a government commission investigating the effects of the Poor Laws found "three generations of the same family simultaneously receiving relief." And, he also pointed out, that after a time it was common for those on welfare to begin to believe that they were entitled to it: " ... the feeling soon became general that pauperism was no disgrace, and the allowance which was obtained from the parish was just as much the rightful property of those who receive it, as the wages of ordinary industry."

Liberal capitalism, in just over two hundred years, has liberated millions from the tyrannies of the past and raised multitudes from poverty. It has also created an arena in which individuals, through their own deeds and accomplishments, could develop senses of self-worth, self-esteem, and the pride that comes from self-responsibility. It is time to permit capitalism to continue its work and extend freedom and prosperity to all of black America between now and the turn of the century. It is time, in other words, to complete the task of extending Adam Smith's system of natural liberty to all Americans and to free them from the new slavery of State dependency.

The papers in this volume, delivered at the sixteenth Ludwig von Mises Lecture Series on April 16 and 17, 1989, are devoted to an analysis of the tragedy that has befallen large segments of black America. The authors come from diverse backgrounds and varying points of view on the political spectrum. What they share in common is a general agreement that fundamental flaws exist in the welfare institutions that have been erected in the last quarter of a century to help the black community. They argue that the economic and social outcome, after twenty-five years, bears little relation to the intentions of those who designed the welfare state. The authors also share a common belief that if real and meaningful improvements are to occur in the black community, it will require radical change. And they also share a common belief that if that change is to occur it will have to come through individual and community initiative, and free market alternatives to government paternalism.

Richard M. Ebeling
Ludwig von Mises
Professor of Economics
Hillsdale College

Contributors

Willie D. Davis

Although he is best known for his decade-long career with the Green Bay Packers and as a Hall of Famer, Willie D. Davis's accomplishments are wide-ranging. An Army veteran and former teacher, he holds an M.B.A. in marketing, personnel management, and industrial relations from the Graduate School of Business at the University of Chicago. He worked as a salesman, then a distributor and director of the Schlitz Brewing Company, and owned his own successful beer distributorship for eighteen years. Currently, he is the owner of All Pro Broadcasting, Inc., with radio stations in Los Angeles, Milwaukee, and Houston. He serves on the board of directors of Fireman's Fund, Sara Lee, Alliance Bank, MGM/UA, K-Mart, and the Dow Chemical Company. Community service has been a hallmark of Mr. Davis's endeavors, from chairing the Los Angeles Urban League to the Boy Scouts, and from directing Junior Achievement to the 1984 Olympic Committee.

Steve Mariotti

Steve Mariotti's work in the inner city has earned him national attention as the president and founder of the National Foundation for Teaching Entrepreneurship which focuses on the needs of handicapped and disadvantaged youths. A former financial analyst at Ford Motor Company and an independent businessman, he became a full-time teacher in the New York City public school system in 1982, teaching in East New York, Bedford-Stuyvesant, Spanish Harlem, the Lower East Side, and the South Bronx, among the nation's most impoverished urban areas. Voted Best Teacher of the Year in 1988 by the 600,000-member National Federation of Independent Businesses, Mr. Mariotti's achievements in the field of free enterprise education have been featured in numerous network news broadcasts, television programs, and national publications.

Charles Murray

Charles Murray is a social scientist and writer. His controversial study of 1960s social policy, *Losing Ground,* has been hailed as "a great book" by the *Wall Street Journal,* called "the Bible of the Reagan Administration" by the *New York Times,* and denounced as a Social Darwinist manifesto by Lester Thurow and John Kenneth Galbraith. Since 1984, it has become virtually obligatory for any book on social policy to begin by stating a position in regards to *Losing Ground*. Dr. Murray has also been recognized as one of the nation's most influential commentators on issues surrounding the underclass and racial polarization. A *U.S. News and World Report* cover story named him among the thirty-two men and women seen as dominating contemporary intellectual debate. A former Peace Corps volunteer, he spent six years in rural Thailand. He has also served as a senior scientist at the American Institutes for Research and he is currently a senior fellow at the Manhattan Institute for Policy Research. His new book, *In Pursuit: Of Happiness and Good Government,* appeared in the fall of 1988.

Paul L. Pryde, Jr.

Paul L. Pryde, Jr., a founding principal of Pryde, Roberts and Company, is an expert in the planning and management of innovative development financing programs. He is nationally recognized as a leader in the design of capital formation strategies for minority and small businesses, especially private-sector ventures to improve the delivery of once-public services. Mr. Pryde received a B.A. in political science from Howard University and has completed graduate studies in business and public administration at George Washington University. He is vice chairman of the Mayor's Economic Development Advisory Committee in Washington, D.C., and chairman of the board of the Corporation for Enterprise Development.

William Raspberry

William J. Raspberry is a columnist for the *Washington Post*. His twice-weekly column is nationally syndicated by the Washington Post Writers Group. Of the columnist, *Time* Magazine has written: "Raspberry has emerged as the most respected black voice on any white U.S. newspaper. He considers the merits rather than the ideology of any issue. Not surprisingly, his judgment regularly nettles the Pollyannas and the militants." He joined the *Post* in 1962 and held a variety of positions until he began his urban affairs column. From 1956 to 1960, he was a reporter-photographer-editor for the *Indianapolis Recorder*. He then served two years in the U.S. Army. In 1965, Raspberry won the Capital Press Club's "Journalist of the Year" award for his coverage of the Watts riots in Los Angeles. He has also received awards from Lincoln University of Jefferson City, Missouri, and the Baltimore/Washington Newspaper Guild.

Walter E. Williams

A professor of economics at George Mason University, Walter E. Williams reaches a broad public through his frequent appearances on programs like

"Face the Nation," "Nightwatch," "Nightline," "Free to Choose," "Firing Line," C-SPAN, and the network news. In the mid-80s he appeared in a WTBS debate series, "Counterpoint," sponsored by the Shavano Institute for National Leadership, opposite socialist leader Michael Harrington. He is also a nationally syndicated columnist for the Heritage Features Syndicate which appears in 90 newspapers around the country. A former professor at Temple University and California State University, a fellow at the Hoover Institution on War, Revolution and Peace, and a staff member of the Urban Institute, Dr. Williams is the author of numerous journal articles and four books: *The State Against Blacks* (1982), *America: A Minority Viewpoint* (1982), *All It Takes is Guts* (1987), and *South Africa's War Against Capitalism* (in press).

Paul L. Pryde, Jr.

How the Black Community Can Invest in its Own Future

About a week after these comments were written, many of America's most prominent black leaders were to assemble in New Orleans to map out a new agenda for black—or, I should say—African-American progress. (I should observe parenthetically that the useful life of any term to describe people of African heritage seems to be twenty years. Being black since about 1968, we were ripe for a style change.)

I sincerely hoped at that time that the ideas that emerged from this conference would be different and more useful than what has historically come out of similar gatherings. I expected, however, to be disappointed. I wrote my predictions accordingly:

> The conference report will probably be very similar to what many of us have seen before. The

first part will be the obligatory litany of despair, a catalogue of the damage done to us by white racism and neglectful government. Here we will hear that conditions in our communities have deteriorated for the twentieth year in a row (surely by now the black community should be close to the U.S. record for most consecutive years of decline).

The second part will be the catalogue of compensatory programs. This will be a laundry list of government spending programs that should be expanded, restored, or created. Little will be said about the need to help African-Americans adapt to the demands of the rapidly changing domestic and international marketplace. Even less will be said about the unprecedented opportunities before us to make these markets work more efficiently and equitably so that all of us can share in the sort of prosperity that is the essence of the American promise.

Well, I *was* disappointed, because that's just what did come out of the conference. I want to share with you here a few thoughts on blacks and markets—why we, as a people, seem to think markets are evil; why, in fact, well-organized capital and labor markets are essential to our economic health; and recognizing that one man's market correction is another's distortion, to offer a couple of suggestions for improving the way capital and labor markets work.

First, what accounts for our market aversion? I think, in large part, it is history. Because of it, we have come to reason as follows:

1. As a result of white malice and inadvertence, American markets have tended to operate in a fashion injurious to our interests.
2. Only when the federal government has intervened to correct the worst abuses of the "free market" have we been able to achieve significant economic progress.
3. Thus markets and those who advocate them are our enemies; and government, and those who advocate it, are our friends.

What we have done is proceed from a pair of generally correct premises to an incorrect conclusion. What we learned is that big government is essential to our well-being. What we should have learned is that government intervention to make markets more efficient and equitable is essential to our progress.

Improving Capital and Labor Markets

To fully appreciate why healthy capital and labor markets are critical to black progress, we must first understand the economic development process. It might be useful to start by saying what it is not. First of all, it is not bricks and mortar. The construction of gleaming new buildings in places that were previously slums may be useful in expanding a city's tax base or in accommodating business expansion. But it is not, in itself, development. Building housing or new commercial facilities to serve a poor community is a good thing to do. But it is not development. Development is not something that is done for or to people. Rather, it is the process by which people, themselves, successfully adapt to economic change.

Second, development is not the same as growth although it helps facilitate the growth that is critical to all our progress. As Roger Vaughan, one of this nation's leading development economists, has put it, growth has to do with *how much* is produced; development, by contrast, with *how* it is produced. Put differently, the process of development involves the creation of economic arrangements and institutions to accommodate needs brought on by economic growth. For example, the entry of women into the workforce has increased the nation's output. It has also helped create a need for a new arrangement for taking care of young children, the day care center. The services of this growing industry not only increase the nation's output, but will, in time, create strains in response to which we will make still other changes in economic arrangements. In other words, growth necessitates development which then leads to further growth.

Like day care, the new economic arrangements which are central to the development/growth spiral generally take the form of new business enterprises, sometimes entirely new industries. Through an analysis of Dun and Bradstreet data, David Birch of MIT found that the disparity between fast-growing and slow-growing areas is accounted for by the difference in business replacement rates. In fast-growing areas, new businesses and industries were born and expanded faster than old ones contracted and died. In slow-growing or declining areas, the reverse was true. It is the difference between San Jose and Detroit.

Research sponsored by the Department of Commerce's Minority Business Development Agency suggests that differential rates of business formation seem to account for disparities in income among different ethnic groups. That research shows a high correlation between a group's business participation rate—the number of businesses per 1,000 of population—and that group's average income. Ethnic or racial groups with the highest business participation rates tend to have the highest average incomes; the groups with the lowest levels of business participation tend to have the lowest average incomes. What this suggests is that entrepreneurship is the engine of development. Through the expansion and creation of new ventures and institutions, successful communities continually adapt to the problems and opportunities created by growth.

Would the U.S. economy flourish without the emergence of the child day care industry and other businesses catering to the needs of working women? How would the U.S. financial system have survived without deposit insurance and how will the old deposit insurance system be changed in response to the emergence of global financial markets?

Entrepreneurship does not, however, flourish without support. We know from academic research and a wealth of practical experience that business formation rates tend to be highest in places and among groups where risk capital is available and lowest where it is not. This brings us back to the importance of efficient markets, in particular, efficient capital markets. After their own savings, most of the money that entrepreneurs obtain to start or expand new companies does not come from government loan programs. Nor should it. Public agencies are very good at solving big problems involving a high degree of standardization. They are abysmal at solving small ones requiring creativity and risk. Instead, risk money for a new firm's inventory, equipment, and working capital comes from friends, family members, and business associates. In other words, it comes from individual savings.

Why Current Capital Markets
Are Not Helping Blacks

Thus, if we want a proliferation of the entrepreneurial events upon which development and growth in the black community depend, it is important that capital markets operate in such a way as to enable new firms that are owned by or employ blacks to attract their fair share of private savings. First, however, we need to know why the nation's capital markets, which are generally regarded as rather efficient, aren't already responding to the needs of emerging firms in the black community.

There seem to be four principal reasons. The first is risk. Firms operating in low-income areas, serving low-income markets, or owned and managed by low-income people are generally regarded to have meager chances for success. Investors will not invest in such firms unless one or more conditions are met. They must be compensated for taking the added risk, or the risk must be reduced, or they must be given information showing that the risk really is not as great as they thought.

This brings us to the second problem, the absence and/or high cost of information about new inner-city or black-owned firms. An investor wishing to purchase the equity or debt of IBM or Texas Air has plenty of sources of inexpensive information on the financial performance and prospects of the firm. He

can read the firm's 10-K, contact the research departments of brokers who trade the company's securities,
or follow the financial page of his newspaper. By contrast, the investor deciding whether to invest in an
inner-city firm may have to go to great lengths and
substantial expense to determine whether the investment is a wise one. Why bother when the likelihood
of an adequate return on capital seems relatively re-
mote?

The third problem is the cost of carrying out the
investment transaction. The investor in Texas Air or
IBM has only to call his broker. The investor in an
unknown black-owned firm must incur the expense
of analyzing an investment proposal, negotiating the
investment contract, and structuring the financing.

Finally, there is public policy. Despite all the talk
about the importance of business formation to the
health of our economy, tax and regulatory policy actually discriminate against investments in entrepreneurship. The Internal Revenue Code is—or at least
used to be—bulging with incentives to invest in real
estate, oil and gas wells, and scores of other capital
assets. Put differently, you can get a tax credit or
deduction if you propose to finance the acquisition
of physical capital. If, however, you want to finance
the human capital of the business—the wages and
training costs of the employees or the learning curve
of the entrepreneur—you are out of luck. In view of
the fact that a significant share of American GNP

growth since World War II can be traced to investments in human capital, this bias is not only unfair but perverse.

How Regulation Stifles Black Entrepreneurship

Financial regulatory policy also discriminates against entrepreneurship and thus against development. Laws restricting the types of assets that commercial banks, pension funds, and insurance companies can own are necessary to protect savers, but they have at least one unfortunate side effect. They discourage investment in the sort of ventures upon which development and growth depend.

In fact, largely because of financial regulation, black America, which badly needs an increase in investment, has become an exporter of capital. Black savings are not invested in black computer companies, day care centers, or retail stores. Through banks, insurance companies, and pension funds, they are invested in orange groves in Florida, shopping centers in Texas, and technology firms in California. I am certainly not proposing that the savings of "widows and orphans" ought to be invested in risky ventures. What I do believe, however, is that we ought to use public policy to correct those "market barriers" that discourage savers who *can* afford to take the risk

of financing investments in black America from doing so.

Proposed Tax Incentives

Of course, I have a modest proposal. The Internal
Revenue Code should be amended to allow any corporation or individual who purchases the equity of a
firm located in a high unemployment area to take a
tax deduction equal to the amount of the purchase.
In addition, any profits from the sale of the investment should be tax-free. In other words, if Mr. Smith
invests $10,000 in his brother-in-law's carpet cleaning
business, he gets to take a $10,000 tax deduction on
that year's tax return. In addition, if Mr. Smith were
to sell the investment a couple of years later for
$15,000, his $5,000 profit would not be taxed. I believe this pair of incentives would have three salutary
development effects.

First, they would encourage increased investment
in qualifying inner-city firms by compensating investors for incurring the increased risk and cost of investing in these firms. To illustrate this point, let's
suppose that the carpet cleaning business is a roaring
success. After five years Mr. Smith's investment is
worth about $25,000, an annual compounded return
of around 20 percent. Let's further suppose that Mr.
Smith is in the 28 percent tax bracket. Under current

tax law, his after-tax return would be about 16 percent. Under my proposal, his rate of return would increase to 28 percent, an increase of a little less than 80 percent.

Second, it would encourage the formation of new financial intermediaries. Most high-income people, the sort who typically purchase tax-advantaged investments, wouldn't think of investing directly in risky companies. Instead, they would prefer to invest through brokers, investment companies, and other intermediaries. The idea I have just described would undoubtedly spur at least some of the nation's financial entrepreneurs to create investment partnerships, blind pools, and various other vehicles to raise money from tax-sensitive individuals and corporations for investment in inner-city firms.

Third, it would stimulate new business formation. As I mentioned earlier, new companies tend to be born and expand in places where there is money to support them. The presence of new sources of capital for young firms would create an environment in which starting a business is seen as a realistic option for significant numbers of people.

The tax incentives I have just outlined should make young, job-creating, inner-city firms more competitive in America's capital market. It is equally important, however, that black workers be competitive in its labor markets. Otherwise, the new jobs created will go to others. What should we do? First, there is one thing we should stop doing and several things we should start doing.

The thing that we must stop doing is supporting, almost reflexively, every government action that imposes new restrictions and costs on employers. While restrictions can keep some bad things from happening, they often produce unintended consequences or prevent useful innovation. For example, a large increase in the minimum wage may seem an unalloyed benefit to black workers. In fact, however, it may increase inflation, thus reducing black purchasing power while conferring most of its benefits on third or fourth wage earners in nonpoor, white families. In addition, it may reduce the number of jobs created by the sort of firms most likely to hire unskilled black youngsters. If we are concerned about increasing the income of black workers, it may be far better to support increases in the earned income tax credit.

As with minimum wage and other laws which increase the cost of labor, we also tend to support laws which require employers to adopt formal hiring policies and procedures in order to limit racial discrimination. While we may think that such laws are without cost, they may also have the unintended consequence of restricting the informal hiring arrangements through which inexperienced black youngsters might receive valuable and marketable work experience. What I am arguing for is not a change in the positions we tend to take, just that more thought be given to them. We must give as much attention to likely effects of changes as to their intentions.

One of the things we need to start doing is demanding more investment in the development of a skilled, literate, and competitive black labor force. To accomplish this, we must change welfare from a system for maintaining the poor into one for making them productive. A number of states have launched experiments in using welfare payments to finance self-employment, training, and support services. I have been working with the National Center for Neighborhood Enterprise on the use of the income from Section 8 housing certificates to finance employment services for public housing residents. Efforts such as these should be expanded and encouraged.

A Restoration of Faith in the Black Community

We must also increase the quality of education and training services by creating marketlike competition between public and private providers. I said earlier that development requires new economic and institutional arrangements. Nowhere is the need more evident than in the way we educate our young and train our workers. Once again, we ought to consider market-oriented methods of financing the needed investment in education and training. Specifically, we ought to consider a new payroll tax, the proceeds of which would be used to finance worker training and retraining. Workers themselves would decide what services to purchase and from whom. After World War II, the G.I. Bill worked well enough. Why not try something similar now?

Likewise, we should consider giving low-income families vouchers for the purchase of education services from both independent and public schools. Experiments in Milwaukee and elsewhere have produced promising results. Certainly, whatever failures we *may* suffer by trying to innovate can be no worse than the failure we will *surely* experience if we do not.

Here is a simple proposition. Development requires investment. Investment requires faith. What I have suggested is that there are ways in which public policy can be employed to make black firms and black labor more attractive and competitive in capital and labor markets. But, there are clear limits to what these changes accomplish, for the willingness to invest is not simply a matter of market structure but of human faith. We may make capital and labor markets work better, but if black America has no faith in its future, no amount of tinkering with taxes and regulation will make a difference.

Walter E. Williams

How Much Can Discrimination Explain?

It would be a mistake to pity blacks as a group of poor, underprivileged people. There is an interesting statistic which contradicts such a notion and testifies to their real success: If you were, for the sake of argument, to consider all black Americans citizens as a separate country and you were to add up all of their earnings, then that country would have (depending on whose data you are using) the ninth to twelfth largest income in the world.

But the black community still faces serious problems. Many of its members are poor and there appears to be little hope for them under the status quo.

The current thinking about civil rights actually hinders black progress. The central premise of the civil rights "vision," *i.e.,* the vision of civil rights organization leaders, judges, lawyers, and bureaucrats, is that statistical disparities in income, occupation, education, and other socioeconomic characteristics are moral injustices caused by an unjust society.

Underlying this premise are several axiomatic assumptions which, if you were to question them, would certainly open you to charges of being uncompassionate and possibly a racist. But question them we must. The first assumption is that discrimination invariably has a negative effect. It is this assumption that forms the justification for the second; that blacks cannot make substantive political, economic, or social progress until discrimination is eliminated. The third assumption is that statistical differences between races are the best measure of discrimination and, furthermore, that if discrimination did not exist, neither would any statistical differences. These assumptions have inspired a considerable amount of litigation as well as employment quotas, minority preferences, busing, and a variety of other race-based policies.

Let's reexamine these assumptions in order to see how valid they are and how much they do tell us about the status quo civil rights vision.

Advancement Despite Discrimination

Does discrimination invariably lead to adverse effects upon its targets? Well, Jews have faced centuries of discrimination which did not end with their emigration to the United States. Yet Jews tend to earn very high incomes and receive a high degree of education—higher in fact than the average American. The Japanese and the Chinese have suffered tremendous discrimination in the United States. At the turn of the century, eleven Western states had statutes prohibiting Asians from owning land. During World War II, Japanese-Americans were interned in American camps, their property virtually confiscated by having to sell quickly at depressed prices. Yet, by every standard of socioeconomic success, Japanese and Chinese rank near or at the top in America. The Japanese enjoy the highest median family income of any group. Twenty-four percent of all Japanese-Americans are skilled or professional workers compared to fourteen percent for the nation as a whole.

Do we have to completely eliminate discrimination in order for a group of people to make broad political, economic, or social progress? If the Jews and the Japanese had waited for such an event, where would they be today? Some might object that Jews are not particularly identifiable so they can simply change their names to avoid discrimination. Well, perhaps some do, but Asians do not have the same refuge.

But those same doubters might claim that blacks have a harder time of it than anybody because of their sad history of slavery. Why then do American blacks of West Indian extraction earn median incomes that are higher than the average American's?

In 1980, 15.6 percent were classified as professional workers. I don't suspect that the average racist takes the time to find out whether a black person is West Indian or a descendant of American slaves before deciding to discriminate against him.

We need not confine our attention to the United States to test this assumption either. Professor Tom Sowell points out in his work that although the Chinese are a minority in Southeast Asia, constituting no more than 12 percent of the population and subject to mass expulsion and massacre over the centuries, they regularly produce the largest percentage of the GNP in nearly every Southeast Asian country. In Malaysia, the figure is in some years as high as 60 percent. The Chinese, in this case, are doing better than the people who are discriminating against them.

In the post-Ottoman Empire, Armenians have faced gross discrimination. In the early part of this century, two million lost their lives at the hands of the Turks. Yet Armenians have incomes much higher than their one-time oppressors.

Statistical Differences: What Do They Mean?

What about statistical differences? Proponents of the status quo civil rights vision would have us believe that, but for discrimination, we would all be equal in nearly every way. We would earn similar salaries and gain similar advancement. We would live in equally distributed neighborhoods and we would all lead proportional lives.

We know that blacks comprise approximately 13 percent of the population. But they represent 75 percent of the professional players in the NBA and are some of the highest paid athletes. How might the civil rights vision explain this anomaly? Do they suggest that blacks are running some kind of conspiracy against the rest of the nation? Is it that the owners of those multibillion-dollar sports businesses are just nice guys, in contrast to their counterparts at Sears and IBM who are ruthless, racist business tycoons?

In the National Hockey League, you would be hard pressed to locate a single black player. Is it because the NHL is basically an evil organization whereas the NBA is not? In professional football, 55 percent of all players are black! In baseball, the figure is near 40 percent.

Sports have other racial disparities. Three of the four highest home-run hitters in major league baseball are black. Of the ten highest batting averages, seven belong to German-Americans. The Most Valuable Player awards nearly always go to blacks, especially in basketball.

What do such statistical differences mean? Do they mean that we must adopt an affirmative action sports policy for Japanese basketball players or black hockey players or white football players? Should we have a quota system for MVP awards?

Racial statistics simply do not mean very much in sports today; performance does. The team owners want the best players. If racial statistics cannot explain much in sports, why should we expect them to explain much in other areas of our lives?

The Truth About Discrimination

All by itself, discrimination cannot explain anything. If you were to ask me what was the cause of the disastrous Grand Hotel fire in Las Vegas a few years ago, I might respond by saying that it was caused by oxygen. After all, no fire can start without oxygen. But if that were the real answer, then why was the MGM Grand Hotel the only one to catch fire? Why didn't the Washington Hilton burn down since it too was surrounded by oxygen?

Discrimination, like oxygen, is everywhere. Every day, we exercise discriminatory habits in the food we eat, the actions we carry out, the thoughts we think. When I chose my wife, I systematically discriminated against all other women. No thought of equal opportunity entered my mind, believe me. In fact, none of the criteria I used in setting up a contractual relationship with my wife met any Equal Opportunity Employment Commission validation criteria. I rejected

Japanese women, white women, women who didn't bathe regularly, women who use foul language, ugly women, women with criminal records ... in short, I rejected all kinds of women. Discrimination is simply choosing between a variety of alternatives.

Please forgive me if I digress and indulge in reciting more statistics: It is commonly argued that since female workers make only 59 cents for every male head of household's dollar in income, then females are unjustly discriminated against. (By the way, single men only make 62 cents for every married man's dollar in income.) However, females who remain unmarried and work continuously from age 18 to 37 actually earn slightly more than males in the same situation. We might urge women that the solution to income differences is not to end discrimination but to end or postpone marriage.

Some Statistics That *DO* Count

There is one valid statistic that *does* help to explain the gap between black and white income. It is group age difference. The median age for all Americans is 32 years old, meaning that half of our population is above that age and the other half is below. Now the median age of Russian Orthodox Jews is 45. The median age of Polish-Americans is 40. The median age of Italians is 34. For Japanese and Italians, it is around 33; for blacks, it is 22; and for Hispanics, it is 16. Should we be surprised or alarmed by significant income differences between groups' statistics when, for example, Hispanics are compared to Italians or Poles? Young people will always earn, as a group, less than mid-career adults no matter what their race or ethnic origin may be.

Age differences help explain other phenomena, too. Crime, for example, is a young man's profession. It is not likely that you are going to find a high crime rate among Russian Orthodox Jews in this country because the general group is older. It is likely that you will find a disproportionate amount of crime among blacks and Hispanics who tend to be much younger.

When I began to write *The State Against Blacks* a number of years ago, many people contended that even if a black man does earn a B.A., he is still going to be discriminated against. The "evidence" was that college-educated black males only make 78 percent of the income of their white counterparts. I decided, therefore, to look at the findings for black female college graduates to see if they suffered similarly. In analyzing census data, I discovered the best-kept secret since the Manhattan Project: in 1975, black female college graduates earned 125 percent of the income of white female college graduates. I compared the distribution of females across 29 different occupations and found black and white females fairly evenly distributed. The biggest category was non-university teaching; about 44 percent of each group fit this description. For black males, non-university teaching was also the biggest category but not for their white counterparts who were mostly engineers. It makes sense then, that there would be a bigger gap between income figures for black and white males, as a group, since engineers made at that time about $8,000 more than nonuniversity teachers. The statistics suggest that even if black and white males were receiving the same wage in each profession, there would be significant differences at the median because blacks have chosen lower-paying professions.

The National Center for Policy Analysis has compiled some revealing statistics which show that black high school graduates who marry, stay married, and work at any kind of job, even at minimum wage, have lower poverty rates. The poverty rate for this group is only slightly over 6 percent. Economists at Ohio State University estimate that if black family structure in America was the same today as it was in the 1950s, the poverty level for blacks would be around 12 percent as opposed to the current 33 percent. The erosion of the family, and the development of high percentages of female-headed households, is a fundamental cause of poverty in the black community.

The illegitimacy rate in places like Harlem, Washington, D.C., and Detroit may run as high as 70 or 80 percent. Whatever the moral implications of this may be, it is clearly bad news from an economic perspective. Imagine you are a black infant whose mother is 15, whose grandmother is 30, whose father is unknown. That's a helluva start in life.

Blacks Finding Their Own Solutions

Rebuilding families is the most important thing blacks can do to raise themselves out of poverty. They can also demand better education through school vouchers or tuition tax credit initiatives which give parents greater schooling choices. Blacks should refuse to tolerate the high levels of crime their youths commit and they should reassume responsibility for the safety of their own neighborhood, even if this means forming neighborhood crime patrols.

Blacks need to be free from the interference of bureaucrats and well-meaning outsiders. Only when blacks find and implement their own solutions to their own problems will they finally join the American mainstream *en masse*.

Charles Murray

Making Good on a 200-Year-Old Promise: Blacks and the Pursuit of Happiness

I am about to give a very gloomy presentation. This is not the message of *Losing Ground* or *In Pursuit*. It is about blacks in America and the nature of their progress or lack of it. I have come to a vision that is so grim that it is almost apocalyptic. It seems to me to be important to examine these issues, however. If the prognosis is bad, let us by all means expose that. Maybe by understanding the problems we can forestall them.

First, some background. In *Losing Ground,* which came out five years ago, I took a nonracial approach which avoided a discussion of racial issues. What I really wanted to do, if I could have gotten the data, was to present what had happened over a period of

time to the poor and disadvantaged in this country
compared to the nonpoor and the nondisadvantaged.
We did not have such a data base, unfortunately, and
so I used as my best approximation a comparison of
blacks vs. whites, saying very explicitly that it must
be irritating to the many blacks who are doing quite
well to be lumped in with the disadvantaged.

Why Racial Difference Theories Fall Short

In subsequent years I have felt vindicated on several counts. One involves my assertion, which I could
only modestly document at the time, that poor whites,
as well as poor blacks, started behaving differently in
the 1960s. A year after *Losing Ground* was published,
I was able to get data from the state of Ohio on the
most explosive issue of all—illegitimate births. The
data demonstrated conclusively that the increasing
problem of births to single women is not occurring
among all socioeconomic groups. It is concentrated
among poor people. This is true of both blacks and
whites. It is not that we have all decided to become
Farrah Fawcett and say that alternative lifestyles are
okay.

Another way in which I feel vindicated in minimiz-
ing racial differences involves jobs. I presented not
an entirely bleak picture in *Losing Ground,* which is to
say I pointed out the many ways in which there had

been dramatic progress among those blacks who got into the labor force. Again, subsequently, I have had a chance to look at that in more detail and once more I am glad to say that there is a variety of reinforcing evidence to that effect, most specifically from the PSID (Panel Study of Income Dynamics) at the University of Michigan. It is fascinating, indeed it is stunning, to realize that in 1970 married black males in the labor force with no more than a high school degree had a poverty rate of only 4%. This figure is far lower than I would have predicted. In this sense (and there is more data to back up this statement), the American dream does work for those who play by certain rules; it works for blacks as for whites, if not perfectly, then at least promisingly so.

The third way I feel vindicated involves the concept of an underclass. It is hard to realize now but when I wrote *Losing Ground* in 1982 and 1983, the word "underclass" was very controversial. At that time, there was a conventional intellectual wisdom that said the only difference between poor people and nonpoor people is that the poor people don't have as much money. Subsequently, "underclass" has not only come into wide use, but there is now widespread recognition that in fact some poor people *are* different; that some are chronically unemployed, chronically on welfare, chronically on drugs or involved in crime. This constitutes a population which is quite different from other low-income people. Finally, consider the issue of why the reforms of the 1960s came about. I argued in *Losing Ground* (following Pat Moynihan, who was one of the first to make this point), that to a great extent the Great Society was born of a white guilt about the way whites had treated blacks for the last 200 years. The guilt was appropriate, but we shouldn't kid ourselves: A great deal of what we did was to help blacks, as opposed to trying to help poor people.

I was struck by the truth of this a few years after *Losing Ground* when I was testifying before the Joint Economic Committee of Congress. I was making the point about the Ohio data on single births I just mentioned—trying to explain that whites have the same behavioral dynamics as blacks do. Another person who was testifying, David Elwood, who has published widely in this area, got quite angry at me. "Everybody knows that's a *black* problem," he said. His anger illustrated, I think, my point that in many ways blacks have been a metaphor in this country for a variety of problems that have very little to do with poverty and a great deal to do with working out white guilt.

Why Treating Groups Differently Is Destructive

In all of these ways I think *Losing Ground* has stood up pretty well. But after this orgy of self-congratulation, I must now confess that I have done a little revisionist thinking, and much of it comes out of the very points I have just made. It has become increasingly clear to me over time that David Elwood was right more profoundly than he knew. Much of what explains American social policy goes back 200 years, driven by a crucial mistake that was made in 1787, when we made up a Constitution that is one of the great creations of mankind, but tried to make this marvelous form of government, so beautifully crafted, coexist with slavery. That fundamental contradiction has so deformed policy ever since, that I think it is in danger now of destroying American democracy—if not within my lifetime, then within the lifetime of my children.

The crucial change, and I think this is a watershed whose importance can scarcely be overestimated, occurred during the mid-1960s and it consisted of this: for the first time, it became legitimate for the federal government to treat different groups of people differently under the law. It is hard sometimes to reconstruct one's own thinking about political matters, but I have a very vivid memory of the summer of 1964 when Congress was debating the Civil Rights Act of that year. I remember thinking that, well, these public accommodation provisions that require people to serve blacks in restaurants, hotels, and so forth were dangerous and pernicious, ultimately, because they gave the government an entry point for interfering in private behavior that it had not had before. But the

nature of the injustice is so egregious that we probably ought to pass the 1964 Civil Rights Act, if we
only add a codicil to it saying, "We're going to do this
one time and we're going to have this law for as long
as we need it, but once people come to their senses
and don't behave as badly as they have we really
ought to take this law off the books because it's so
dangerous." I was only 21 at the time, and maybe I
can be forgiven for not realizing that it doesn't work
that way. Once government gets its foot in the door,
the situation gets constantly worse. What started out
as a bill that was trying to make a few simple changes
in a few outrageously discriminatory behaviors became subsequently an affirmation of the legitimacy
of treating different people in different ways as long
as your motives were good. What was a bill that origi-
nally tried to have equal treatment for groups subsequently became what we know as "strong affirmative
action," meaning a kind of quota system.

I am not so worried about the actual legislation on
this regard as I am about the intellectual acceptance
of the notion that treating people as groups is okay.

Education

I will use education as an example because I think
it is the most obvious one. Every year about 25,000
white students score in the 700s on the math portion
of the SAT test. The number of blacks who score in

the 700s in math are in the dozens—about 200, usually. Because of strong affirmative action, the elite colleges aggressively go out to recruit minority students for their classes. They are exceedingly successful. I have been told by a Harvard faculty member who does not want to be identified, but who has had access to the admissions data, that the Harvard freshman class typically takes in 50% of all black students in the nation who score in the 700s on either the verbal or math sections of the SAT. That's one school. Add in Princeton and MIT and Stanford and a few other schools, and you have pretty well soaked up not only that batch but also a very high proportion of the blacks who scored in the 600s.

The first problem this raises has to do with black students themselves. Consider MIT as an example. At MIT, the average incoming black student scores in the top 10% of all students in the math SAT—not the top 10 percent of MIT students, but *all* students in the United States. This means that these are real smart kids. The average white or Asian in the MIT freshman class, however, is in the top 1% or top 1/10 of 1%. What happens is not all that hard to predict. If you are a black freshman, you arrive at MIT as a successful person: you know you're smart, you know you're able, you're looking forward to this experience, and yet you soon find yourself at the bottom of your class. And if you don't think that has devastating psychological effects, the dropout rate at MIT, despite intensive efforts to keep minority students, is 24%, compared to half that for whites. And this is 24% of a population that should be spectacularly successful. That's the effect on black students.

The effect on white students is much worse. Harvard and MIT and Princeton and Yale act as a very efficient vacuum cleaner. A lot of the black students who should have been studying engineering at Purdue or Iowa State, and would have been very successful there, are not at Purdue—they are at MIT. Meanwhile, Purdue and Iowa State are trying to get whatever black students they can get (they are treating groups differently for their own good, naturally) and here's what happens.

The white student population going into those schools is dangerously innocent. By dangerously innocent, I mean that racism really doesn't make sense to a lot of young people these days. In one sense I am very happy to see that. My nineteen-year-old daughter simply cannot imagine why people would be racist because it's so silly. But with this innocence goes a problem that is not unlike a failure to be vaccinated when in an area where a disease is still prevalent. So these innocents get to their classroom in their college and they look around at the white kids in the class and their performance, and they look around at the black kids in the class and their performance. And the empirical fact is that among the white students, they see dumb kids, smart kids—they see the entire range. Among the black students, they have a much more truncated range in their classroom because of the phenomenon I have been talking about. Now, everything would be fine if the white students would then say, "The reason we have this situation is because of an artificially truncated recruitment market." But they don't do that. Too often what they tend to do is say, "Gee, blacks must not be as smart as whites." When I look at rising racial tensions around the campuses in the United States, I would argue that it is not the old-fashioned redneck racism that is the driving force here. I think the driving force is self-righteous kids who think that their hearts are pure as the driven snow in terms of racism, who are making empirical judgments about their local situations and coming to these conclusions. The old virus is starting to take hold.

The Job Market

What I have said about education is also true in the job market. I'll give you a quick example using myself. I went through MIT as a graduate student. I loved computer programming, still do. I can spend hours on end with a computer writing a program and debugging it; it is great fun. There's only one problem. I'm not real good at it. It's like chess: At a certain level, I can play a decent game of chess, but not nearly as good as I should play considering the amount of time I've spent on it. I don't have a knack for it. At MIT, I was not in any danger of being recruited by IBM at a fancy salary to be a computer programmer. And because I was in no danger of that, I was in no danger of getting into programming as a career. And since there were other things I did pretty well, I went out and did those instead. But if I had been black with an MIT Ph.D. and my level of programming skill, I would have gotten those fancy offers, because IBM is hungry for black Ph.Ds. And I would have gone into a career in which I was mediocre, passing up careers in which I could have done much better. This story has nothing to do with racial differences and everything to do with the way in which society has been structured.

The Underclass

The things I have said are bad enough in themselves, but they become especially dangerous when we conjoin what I consider to be a rising tide of racism driven by strong affirmative action with the underclass problem. For a long time, there has been an intellectual conventional wisdom about the underclass which said that the reason why we observe these problems is because of structural unemployment which means that there just aren't jobs available out there, or if there are jobs, they are too low-paying to attract people, or the jobs are out at the edge of the city where people can't get to them. But in several cities around the country we have now watched four or five years of very tight labor markets, and what we have seen is unemployment drop dramatically among blacks as well as whites. But that refers to people in the labor market. People in the labor market are not creating an underclass. If you ask about people *not* in the labor market, the answer is that tight labor markets have had no appreciable effect.

For many years, the intellectual conventional wisdom has also held that social programs will work if we only intervene actively enough to solve all sorts of problems that characterize the underclass. Here, too, a change is occurring. There are still people who say I was too pessimistic in *Losing Ground,* but there are fewer than there used to be, and the number of people who are skeptical about the ability of social programs to make major changes in the lives of people is growing.

Add into this changing intellectual scene a few other factors—such as, for example, AIDS, which, within the next few years, is going to be very specifically identified as a disease of the underclass. Gay infections are leveling off. The educational process in the gay community has been very effective, the organizational process has been effective, and behavioral changes have occurred. But among IV drug users, the hardest population to reach with educational measures, we have seen the least effect. We are going to have a continuing rising rate of infection. The exact size of that infection rate is unknown at this point, but it is large enough to be frightening even given the data we have. We are seeing percentages like 5 and 10 percent of males coming to inner-city emergency rooms who are infected. Now even if we say that that is too high to be a good estimate for the inner-city population as a whole, it is still so high as to be staggering. If you assume these rates continue to increase for a few more years, I think you are going to find that the white population gets increasingly scared of the inner cities—and they are already pretty scared because of crime. And the white population is also going to be much less empathetic than in the past. For some time, almost all of us had to say to ourselves, "there but for the grace of God go I"—insofar as no one could know that this thing called AIDS was lurking out there. But now we do know, and people who continue to get the disease are getting it because they are doing things that they should know better than to do. A lot of the empathy for their plight is thus going to disappear.

A Crisis in the Making

Put all these things together. Add up the increasing evidence that lack of jobs is not the problem in unemployment, add the pessimism about social programs, consider the fear of the inner city that is already evident (and it is going to get worse). Add to that a few other factors such as the baby boomers turning forty and becoming more conservative in many ways. You mix all that together, and then finally you add in that it is legitimate to treat different groups of people differently with the apparatus of the state, and you have an explosive situation. I cannot predict exactly how the situation is going to play out. I am in the position of an analyst in Weimar, Germany, in the early 1920s saying, "We've got a real problem with anti-semitism," without being able to predict Dachau. I assert that we have a crisis in the making, without knowing what form it will take. Even now one hears sotto voce or after a few drinks at a cocktail party, among quite liberal people, all sorts of things being said about the underclass which they most definitely would not want to have associated with their name in the columns and books they usually write. They are willing to say certain things in private now; those views are eventually going to come out into the open. Once they do, other measures that are now not even considered will become more readily conceivable. I am thinking of possibilities ranging from more state intervention into who can have children and who cannot, to a more general situation in which we treat the inner city like we treat Indian reservations.

I told you it was going to be an apocalyptic speech. The reason it is apocalyptic for all of us, not just the blacks in the inner city, is that we cannot have a democracy in which a large portion of the population is deemed unfit to participate. If you treat a large portion of the population as wards of the state in this fashion, I think you have introduced a fundamentally crippling dynamic.

Self-Government for the Inner Cities

The way out of this is hard to see because I see so little enthusiasm for radical change, but I will tell you what I think the radical change must be. We must affirm the American experiment using the bedrock Jeffersonian principle of self-government: that all people, of a wide variety of personalities and intelligences and abilities, are able to govern themselves, given only a framework in which the government protects the citizens who live within it from being preyed upon by each other. My proposition is that giving self-government to the inner cities is not only a feasible way of dealing with the problem, it is the only way.

By giving the inner city self-government I mean very simple things, such as giving control of the schools back to parents in the inner city, based on the assumption that most parents want good things for their children. Most parents are able to identify what they want in their schools; some not very exotic things such as good discipline, demanding curricula, demanding tests. That is true of poor black people in the inner city as well as whites out in the suburbs. If you left the control of schools in the hands of parents in the inner cities, do you really think they would come up with anything that looks remotely like the school systems that are in place right now? Tuition tax credits or vouchers are my favorite way of giving control to parents, but it can be done in a variety of other ways as well.

Give control of law enforcement and criminal justice back to the inhabitants of the inner city. For example, suppose that we make one simple change: from now on, everyone who is arrested for a felony is tried by a jury of his peers drawn from within a four-block radius of where the crime was committed. What do you think the decisions of those juries would be? What do you think the effect on control of the neighborhood would be?

The middle class can do its part by providing the money to house the people that are judged to be unfit to walk in the streets of the inner city. Now I understand that in recommending this I am being a Neanderthal. Lest anyone think that I am in favor of just building more prisons, I am all in favor of things like halfway houses and other less restrictive options—with one proviso. Let's build all the halfway houses in middle-class suburbs instead of in poor neighborhoods. The middle class can decide where it wants to put these folks that the inner city doesn't want on the streets, but let's at least perform the primary function of government for these communities by keeping them safe.

Lastly, I would give self-government to the inner city in terms of dealing with its families and its children. Communities are vital insofar as they have functions to perform and the main functions involve the family and care of children. Discouraging young women from having children that they are not prepared to take care of is not a matter of money. It is a matter of messages that can only be conveyed by people who are in the immediate geographic neighborhood. The way to get those messages conveyed is by giving control back to that neighborhood, meaning decentralization of all the welfare functions—and their costs, now lodged in municipal and federal agencies.

There is not a snowball's chance in hell of any of this happening in the foreseeable future. But I am quite serious when I say that half measures are not going to work in this case. And if there is not a chance of enacting these steps in the immediate future, we at least ought to start entertaining the thought, because thinking about them is the essential first step. I suggest to you that, above all, we consider how unradical the solution is, in this sense: What I am proposing for the inner city is no more than what you want for yourselves.

Willie D. Davis

Positioning for Excellence in a Color-Blind Market

I am by no means an authority on all the aspects of black economic progress in America, but I would like to share several experiences which have given me the chance to become personally involved with such progress and to see its impact on others.

Having spent my early career in professional football, I am constantly reminded of the fact that in the business world you still have to look out for the blind-side block. You are never safe, in athletics or business; yet I think it is proper to say that in recent times, athletics may be much safer! When it comes to developing commercial products, it is not unusual for an enterprising businessman to invest millions of dollars in a new item only to find that Ralph Nader is his first customer.

Well, there is something rather frightening and humbling about that, as you can well imagine. Anyone going into business has to be committed to looking over his own shoulder to see what's behind him— that's the only way to position for excellence in the color-blind market.

What do I mean by the color-blind market? Clearly, you can assume that in such a market one is unable to enjoy unusual opportunities or advantages because of one's race. Discriminating factors do not apply. I am not suggesting this market exists completely today—but it is coming and blacks, particularly, need to think long and hard about such a prospect.

Changing Market Strategies

There are many developments today which will revolutionize the way products are marketed and which will indeed change the way we live our lives. When it comes to the factors we most often think of in marketing, they will become more general and broad-based, appealing to a wider range of consumers.

Take, for instance, black hair care products that started out with a very specific market—now there are lots of cross-over products and hair care products for all types of people. A market can start out one way and then change direction.

It is important to realize that products that started out with some limited but proprietary advantage are more and more being handled as commodities for expanded consumption. One of the fastest-growing industries that has undergone such a transformation is that of the computer industry.

Computers were once exorbitantly expensive, complicated, and dependent on a lot of hardware and software. They were not, in short, for everybody. But now there are dozens of affordable, relatively simple computer systems to be had for every conceivable use.

To return to market strategies. Historically, demographics have, more or less, been the basis for most marketing decisions—age, sex, household income, education, geographic location—and these sorts of things. Then along came a little "race" and a little "origin" and a few "cultural experiences." But the positioning and advertising of products is changing. I contend that positioning in the future will be based more on the value-added concept, on product benefits, and product "fit"; in other words, how well a product can satisfy the need that a consumer has decided is most important.

The most compelling case I would make for the whole idea of a color-blind market emanates from my broadcasting experience. Twelve years ago when

I bought my first radio station, I played black artists 99 percent of the time, and I felt that I was serving the interest of the black audience that I intended to serve and that gave me my niche in the marketplace. Today, that same radio station is featuring black artists only 70 percent of the time and is offering major advertising geared to all consumers, regardless of race. The marketplace has to a great extent become indifferent to whether or not a recording artist is black.

Is this wrong? I would never be the one to make such a claim. Is there something to feel a little bit disappointed about? Possibly, but whether we accept it or not, this is the kind of marketplace we are headed for in the future. I am very concerned that all entrepreneurs, minority or otherwise, be prepared to cope with such a business environment. They must be prepared to say "let's do it well enough to survive under all conditions."

This is the color-blind market at work, and it is a market that is far more rational than emotional in its structure. It is in this area where most adjustment will occur, especially on the entrepreneurial side of marketing. Once you have decided that you have a great idea, you take it to the marketplace expecting to enjoy success. You may indeed do so, or you may simply find there are no takers. Why? Because the market has demonstrated that there is no need or there is no desire for it. A product succeeds or fails on its own merit.

An End to Minority Preference Legislation

But I think that another important aspect of marketing in the future could very well be influenced by the legal interpretation of the law as it relates to minorities. Minority preferences, for example, have been a very important factor to the FCC. They often use race and gender as the criteria to decide who should be given a "frequency" in the radio and television industry. Due to several recent Supreme Court cases, what was once an apparent FCC mandate to create a preference in allocating licenses to females and other minorities is no longer enforceable. Indeed, the notion of "compensatory justice," in the sense of what takes place in the future to right any perceived past wrong, is in question. Minority set-aside contracts and many other current business practices in which minority preference has been exercised are on the way out.

Can you imagine, at this point in time, that racism or any form of documentable disadvantage could successfully prove the need for minority preference in the marketplace? I would say it is very unlikely, especially in light of the position the courts seem to be taking. In the past, the greatest protector of minorities have been activists, public interest groups, and the academic community. But their role is changing, too. The challenge is to insure that equal access will continue to exist for minorities under the new color-blind rules that are slowly taking shape.

I had the opportunity recently to speak to a group of black MBA students at the University of Chicago, and one of the things I pointed out to them was that eighteen years ago when I went into Watts, California, and started a beverage company, I had every expectation that it would be smooth sailing. Watts had a population that was 90 percent black, and I would be able to attach my name to a national product that would appeal to them because I was a black myself. Well, I assure you that it was one of those rare cases where expectations come true. But, five years later, other manufacturers and distributors were sponsoring other minority distributors. And all at once there was no real reason why all the black retailers in south central Los Angeles felt they had a compelling reason to do business with the Willie Davis Distributing Company. "Okay," I said, being a competitor all my life, "I'll handle this." And I managed to survive. But shortly after that, a plethora of imports, European imports to be specific, hit the market. I said, "Gee, I didn't plan on this one." But I managed to survive again. Then, lo and behold, along came wine coolers and a number of other derivative products that all at once made this market far more complex, far more competitive than the original market I walked into. Virtually all I had to do years ago was to go in and ask for the business and it was given to me. The beverage business I went into two decades ago is simply a different business today and I could not survive walking into that same marketplace today with the attitude I had then.

Liability and Global Competition

Some people used to argue that greater liability would ultimately produce greater products. That may be true to some extent—some products may be better, but indeed there are far fewer products on the market as a result. In the chemical industry, pesticides and contraceptives are pretty much at a standstill. As I look at something as dear to me as sports, I can see what "liability" has done. When I became a football player, there were probably twenty helmet manufacturers in business. Today there is only one.

Expanded product liability has also created a serious problem for this country in its struggle to remain competitive with foreign countries where the laws are infinitely more liberal in their interpretation of product liability. Product innovation is essential in order to compete in the global market, but in the last few decades changes in the area of liability have created excessive legal action and eliminated many worth-while goods and services. It has also hamstrung the development of new products. "Why bring out a product if it could ultimately land me in court?" says the would-be entrepreneur.

But it will be the world market, in my opinion, that will force greater acceptance of risk in the market-place.

Perhaps the most significant of all the factors which are creating a new kind of market, and the one that I would characterize as indifferent, is global competi-tiveness. We no longer have local protected markets. We compete in an international market.

When I first signed with a pro football team, coaches and managers said to the new players, "You just joined one of the finest football organizations in the world. You've got to think of this team as the IBM, the AT&T, and the General Motors of the sport." And when I first went into business, the first thing I heard from many corporate leaders was, "We think of ourselves as the New York Yankees, the Bos-ton Celtics, and the Green Bay Packers of the busi-ness world." Clearly, there is admiration for excel-lence wherever it exists. People like to associate them-selves with it. But the most interesting thing, even though some corporations and teams are not always riding the wave of success, they still strive to maintain an image and a reputation of excellence. They want to sustain it within their organization through good times and bad. One of today's more perplexing problems is doing the same thing in the marketplace. Entrepreneurs need to ask themselves, "How do we do our business with a greater responsibility to those things that have been proven to be good in terms of image and reputation?" They must address the "empty promise." Too often, today, empty promises abound. How many times have you watched television and were convinced to buy a product which later failed to live up to its promise? That is the problem of advertising claim vs. real experience and it leads to a kind of pervasive climate of unfulfilled expectations. Unfulfilled expectations soon become the norm and that is the problem I think we must avoid whether we are dealing with a color-blind or any other market.

Regarding my own definition of competitiveness, I always consider the process of elimination important. Competition in its purest form is simply letting excellence prevail as inefficient, less-qualified companies fall off the chart. That is one of the realities we must learn to live with. And it is one of the reasons why I feel very sure that the color-blind, global market of the future will indeed be one driven more by economics, by price, by convenience, and by added-value than by anything else. Such a market will be healthy for all companies.

Many things served me so well in athletics that I have tried to carry them with me all the rest of my life. One is the conviction that what drives small companies into major successful corporations are good individuals within that company. How do you encourage these people? When I was with the Green Bay Packers, Vince Lombardi talked about something called good habits. "What," I asked him, "does this have to do with blocking and tackling?" He replied that the reason he wanted me and the other Green Bay Packers to have good habits is because habits, good or bad, soon become the natural thing to do. One of the things that has hurt American business is its tendency to drift away from the basics, the fundamentals. We must make sure that we are indeed dealing with the fundamentals that are essential to operating and managing our businesses, and that we develop good habits and good examples. Americans are fortunate to be able to boast of so many great leaders over the years; we should all learn from them.

Ultimately our economy is driven by pride and performance. With a color-blind market, these factors will be doubly important.

Steve Mariotti

Generating Entrepreneurial Activity in the Inner Cities: Hope for the Future

For the past six years, I have been trying to become an expert in a neglected field—that of teaching entrepreneurship and basic free market economics to inner-city black, Hispanic, and disadvantaged youths. My interest in this field came about under unusual circumstances.

Seven years ago, I was a small businessman with an import-export firm on New York's Lower East Side. One day I went out for a jog and was mugged by four inner-city kids. It was very like the experience of Bernhard Goetz; they approached me and demanded money—five or ten dollars. I didn't have the money and I asked them to go away. I was assaulted. Needless to say, it was a very traumatic experience.

But while I was recovering, I began to think about the incident from a different perspective. If those kids had come to me for a $10 loan, or had they had something legitimate to sell me, or had they wanted me to invest in a business, I probably would have given them the money. I was troubled that they had to resort to violence when they could have been making a sales pitch.

Putting Entrepreneurship into the Curriculum

I thought about this for about six months, and I began writing letters and making phone calls to a variety of people. What I discovered was that there was virtually nothing being done in order to get inner-city youths involved in business. As you may know, most high school business departments are controlled by typing teachers, so the majority of students go through four years of education without getting any information about finance, marketing, or product development, much less basic economic principles.

So I decided to make a career change. I approached the New York City school board and introduced myself. I requested assignments in the most difficult neighborhoods, and once I was there, I asked for the "worst" students. Of course, I was labelled a nut; after all, there are a lot of schools in New

York where teachers just won't go voluntarily, and lots of "worst" students every teacher wants to avoid. At a school where I was assigned early on, Boys and Girls High School, which lies at the heart of Brooklyn's Bedford-Stuyvesant area, there were 48 physical assaults in one year, and that was typical. I taught in schools around the New York City area for six years, but I couldn't convince a single principal to endorse my work or approve a plan for students to start their own companies. I couldn't get any financing either. Administrators cited fears about handling money, about holdups, liability, and that sort of thing.

Then, finally, I met a remarkable woman in the section of South Bronx called Fort Apache, generally considered the most dangerous area of the city. Her name is Patricia Black and she is the principal of Jane Addams Vocational High School. From our first meeting, she gave her full support to my plan and she put me in charge of the business department in the field of special education.

Special Ed Students

Special ed students have a great many problems dealing with the world around them and they often don't function very well in a structured environment. But I enjoy working with them because I believe they are indeed special and that God has granted them special gifts to offset their problems. Sometimes, it is just that they don't fit into the conventional hierarchy of traditional education; Henry Ford and Ray Kroc were such special ed students.

To date, about three hundred students have gone through the program which includes learning all the basic steps of starting and running a small business as well as the fundamentals of a market economy. The companies these students formed have earned more than $100,000 in sales in just the last two years.

The Influence of Ludwig von Mises

None of this would have been possible without the help of Barbara Bell and Raymond Chambers of the Boys and Girls Club of Newark (which is doing some of the best educational work in the inner-city today). In addition, I founded my own nonprofit group, the National Foundation for Teaching Entrepreneurship. But it also wouldn't have been possible, for me, at least, without an introduction to the writings of one of the great minds of this century, Ludwig von Mises.

When I was sixteen years old, I was a socialist, to the horror of my relatives, especially my grandfather, Lowell R. Mason, a well-known libertarian attorney. He sent me a copy of Mises's monumental study, *Hu-*

man Action, with a note that said that if I read the book and wrote a report on it, he would pay me $100.

Well, that was the most valuable job I ever had. I will never forget the experience of finding out about the way the free market works. The effect on my thinking was revolutionary. Within a matter of weeks, I went from looking at life as a totalitarian to a classical liberal. The insights of Ludwig von Mises, whom the *Champions of Freedom* series honors, have helped me accomplish what amounts to pioneering work in the inner cities.

What is really ironic, however, is that with all the emphasis on the study of entrepreneurship which goes on at the college level in America, and with the worldwide intellectual movement toward classical liberalism, Ludwig von Mises's name is rarely mentioned outside of places like Hillsdale College. Of all the "crimes" of academia which can be attributed to Keynesian socialism and communism, one of the greatest is that the Austrian school of economics has never gotten the credit it deserves. My debt to Ludwig von Mises and his followers, like my old friend Richard Ebeling who now holds the Mises chair at Hillsdale, is incalculable. And so is my debt to Hillsdale College, which I consider to be one of the finest liberal arts schools in this country. This school, with its dedication to human liberty—both political and economic—is a beacon to all of those who must stand alone in defense of freedom.

The Program's Results

There are six basic findings which I have discovered in teaching free enterprise and entrepreneurship to inner-city youths.

Improved Attitude

The first finding is that the students who go through the program display marked improvement in their general attitude and their level of courteous behavior toward others. A big problem with inner-city students is that they can be very, very rude.

But when a student is treated well and, moreover, treated as a professional entrepreneur, he begins to act the role. It reminds me of a scene from *One Flew Over the Cuckoo's Nest* in which Jack Nicholson and a group of inmates escape from an insane asylum. When the police catch up with them and ask who they are, Nicholson answers, "We're doctors." He introduces the inmates who begin to act just like doctors.

Yet it is still difficult to work with special ed students who are severely troubled. The threats, the swearing, the anti-social behavior used to bother me a great deal and it is natural to become worn out in such a situation. Then about three years ago, I began to pay attention to a condition I hadn't really considered before: "post-traumatic stress disorder." Rape victims, abused children, Vietnam veterans, those who have suffered from an automobile accident or other injury may have such a condition. When a person is subjected to very intense stress, especially over a long period of time, the brain may undergo chemical changes. I suspect that many special ed students in the inner city exhibit post-trauma behavior or an ongoing traumatic stress disorder.

A few statistics help tell the story. Of every 21 black teenagers who are now 13, one will be murdered by the age of 20. In some Newark neighborhoods, the figure is closer to one out of every 13 and in Detroit it is one in 10. (Keep in mind that during World War II, the Russians lost about one-tenth of their population and you will have an idea of the kind of carnage this represents.) It is not hard to believe that growing up in the inner city is traumatic and that inner-city kids may have a great deal of trouble with social relations and in school.

Improved Academic Skills

The second major finding is that many inner-city students who have never learned basic math have an incentive to do so when running their own business. By basic math, I don't mean algebra or geometry, but addition, subtraction, and multiplication. The average student in our program sees his or her math skills improve from a second-grade to a seventh-grade level in less than a month—that is the highest level Winston Churchill ever achieved, and it is about all most people ever need. Their communication skills are also refined and they learn how to read better and to follow instructions carefully.

Developing Initiative

The third finding is that the program draws on the students' natural inclinations toward entrepreneurship. They develop the ability to take risks; they develop initiative; they develop mental toughness. This is important because it provides a glimmer of hope for our inner cities, all of which—whether it be Washington, D.C., the South Bronx, the South Side of Chicago, Watts, or Detroit—have seen their problems become significantly worse: rising murder rates, teenage pregnancy, drug abuse, violence, crimes against people and property. The catalyst for turning things around is this group of kids I work with. Even growing up with tragedy all around them, they can develop entrepreneurial skills. They have no fear in sales; they get knocked down, but they come right back. This is a positive trait that can be developed in legitimate ways.

Reduced Pregnancy Rate

The fourth finding surfaced only a few year ago. I was teaching typing and entrepreneurship at the same time and on one occasion when I was grading the students' work, I started circling the names of pregnant teenage girls in the typing classes as opposed to those in the entrepreneurship classes. The ratio was three to one! I went over my old records and was amazed that I hadn't noticed this trend before, but it was clear.

The young women who had been exposed to the concept of creating a business were much less likely to get pregnant. Giving them a vision, a long-term goal, and a sense of self-esteem through their own success are the keys that the entrepreneurship classes provide and this is critical when you realize that half of all inner-city women, who are largely black or Hispanic, will become pregnant before the age of 20. Of this number, half will give birth, so for every 100 inner-city teenagers, 25 will have at least one child and 90 percent will be born out of wedlock. (To be honest, I question the 90 percent; during all my years in the New York inner-city school system, I have seen hundreds of pregnant girls and am aware of only two who married.)

The Adverse Effect of Regulation

The fifth finding is that government regulation, particularly in regard to entrepreneurial activity, can have a significant adverse effect. It is an established classical economic principle that there are costs to any form of government intervention in the marketplace.

As has been pointed out by many free-market economists, these costs usually fall on people who have little or no financial capital. Wealthy and middle-class targets can hire lawyers and accountants to shield themselves; the poor cannot. When the government makes it difficult to start a business by adding regulations or paperwork to the process, poor and low-income people in the inner city give up.

"Ideas Have Consequences"

The sixth finding relates to a well-known concept: "ideas have consequences," but it needs to be applied more often to inner-city problems. Most people are negative about the inner city and blame lack of funds or some other cause. But it is in the realm of ideas where we need to look for help.

Look at the remarkable transformation that has taken place in modern Japan. In the 1950s to 1960s, "Made in Japan" was synonymous with junk. Japanese goods stood for cheap and shoddy workmanship. But then an Oklahoma professor by the name of Deming went to Japan and introduced a thirteen-point program on quality control. These points were just basic ideas, but the Japanese took them very seriously and today "Made in Japan" stands for excellence.

Inner-city entrepreneurship is an idea that can have consequences just as dramatic. I am optimistic about the future. I think that we are within a generation of a renaissance in our inner cities. There is nothing wrong with inner-city youths—they surely prove that ideas have consequences and that we ought to redouble our efforts to share the right kind of ideas with them as they are growing up.

William Raspberry

A Journalist's View
of Black Economics

Let me begin by clearing the air of false expectations. Like the other contributors to this volume, I
am intensely interested in the subject of the economics of black America. Unlike the others, however, I
am neither a businessman, an economist, nor a social
scientist. I'm a newspaper guy.

That's not an apology. I like being a newspaper
guy, and I like to think I'm a pretty good one. I point
it out simply to warn you up front that what you will
hear from me is neither economic analysis nor nuts-
and-bolt business proposals. Since nobody has told
me otherwise, I will assume that I was invited to come
here because I like to think about things. My proposal
is that we spend the next several minutes thinking
about things together.

Myths About Race

One of the things I would like us to think about is a myth: a myth that has crippled black America, sent us off on unpromising directions, and left us ill-equipped to deal with either political or economic reality.

That myth is that race is of overriding importance, that it is a determinant not just of opportunity but also of potential; a reliable basis for explaining political and economic realities, a reasonable way of talking about geopolitics, and the overwhelming basis on which to deal with the relationships between us.

When I refer to race-based explanations of the plight of black America as myth, I do not mean to suggest that all such explanations are false. My reference is to the definition of myth as a "traditional account of unknown authorship, ostensibly with a historical basis, but serving usually to explain some observed phenomenon."

The historical basis of our preoccupation with race is easy enough to see. America did not invent slavery. Slavery as an institution predates the Bible. But American slavery was peculiarly race-based. Since slavery is the basis for the very presence of black people in America, small wonder that race has assumed such importance in our mythology.

But slavery was more than just involuntary, unpaid servitude. Unlike other populations, to whom enslavement seemed a reasonable way of dealing with conquered enemies, America was never happy with the concept of one group of human beings holding another group of human beings in bondage. I suppose it was taken as a sin against God. But rather than forgo the economic benefits of slavery, American slaveholders resolved the dilemma by defining blacks not as fellow human beings but more like beasts of burden. There is nothing ungodly about a man requiring unremunerated work of an animal. Didn't God give man dominion over the animals?

Now it may have been that Africans were a special kind of animal: capable of thought, and human language, and even worship. But as long as whites could persuade themselves that blacks were not fully human, they could justify slavery.

Thus was born and reinforced the myth of inherent white superiority, which later became the basis for racial separation, for Jim Crow laws, for unequal opportunity and all sorts of evil. Nor is it just among whites that the myth survives.

I must say that this fact never really hit home for me until a few years ago when a reader of my column suggested it. Mary Pringle, a Virginia educator, said it occurred to her that Americans generally have lost the myths that give meaning to their lives, and that black Americans in particular suffer from the loss. The predominant surviving myth of black Americans, she said, is that of racism as the dominant influence in their lives.

Myths, she was careful to point out, are not necessarily false. Indeed, whether positive or negative, they are almost always based on actual group experience. But the nature of the operative group myth can make a profound difference in group outcomes.

"Racism is a reality, but it has been overcome by many and given way to opportunity and success." Those who have overcome it, she argued, have been moved by different myths: myths that paint them as destined for success rather than doomed to failure, myths that lead them to see themselves as members of a special group capable of overcoming all odds. That is the kind of myth that blacks need to cultivate, she said.

"Racism, though it is a reality, has been a destructive myth, giving greater power to the odds against success than exist in reality, making it harder even to *try*. What we need is a stronger, more powerful myth that is constructive and evokes a sense of identity and energy to move ahead."

I think Mary Pringle's insight is profound. As with most keen insights, once it occurs to you, you can see supporting evidence on every hand.

Black youngsters in the inner cities are moved by the myth that blacks have special athletic gifts, particularly with regard to basketball. Asian youngsters are influenced by the myth that they have special gifts for math and science. Jewish youngsters accept the myth that their group has a special gift for the power of the written word.

Now all these myths are, by themselves, worthless. But when they evoke a sense of identity and the energy to move ahead, something happens. People *work* at the things they believe they are innately capable of achieving.

So it is not uncommon to see a black kid working up to bedtime, practicing his double-pump scoop, his behind-the-back dribble, his left-handed jump shot. And after a few months of work, if he has any athletic talent at all, he *proves* the myth. Asian-American youngsters, convinced that they may have special aptitude for math or science, reinforce that myth and make it reality—staying up until two in the morning working on their math and science; Jewish youngsters, convinced that they have a special gift for the written word, work at writing.

Those are all positive myths, and they are obviously powerful. But negative myths are powerful, too.

The myth that blacks cannot prevail in intellectual competition, that Chinese youngsters cannot play basketball, that Jews are specially vulnerable to guilt trips—these are negative myths whose acceptance has led to failure because they feed the assumption that failure is inevitable.

Objective reality is the arena in which we all must perform. But the success or failure of our performance is profoundly influenced by the attitudes—the myths—we bring to that reality.

Two things flow from the racism-is-all myth that we have used to account for our difficulties. The first is that it puts the solution to our difficulties outside our control. If our problems are caused by racism, and their solutions dependent on ending racism, our fate is in the hands of people who, by definition, don't love us.

A Skewed Definition of Civil Rights

The second outcome of the myth is our inclination to think of our problems in terms of a failure of racial justice. "Civil rights," which once referred to those things whose fair distribution was a governmental responsibility, now refers to any discrepancy. Income gaps, education gaps, test-score gaps, infant-mortality gaps, life-expectancy gaps, employment gaps, business-participation gaps—all now are talked about as "civil rights" issues.

The problems indicated by all these gaps are real. But describing them as "civil rights" problems steers us away from possible solutions. The civil rights designation evokes a sort of central justice bank, managed by the government, whose charge is to ladle out equal portions of everything to everybody. It prompts us to think about our problems in terms of inadequate or unfair distribution. It encourages the fallacy that to attack racism as the source of our problems is the same as attacking our problems. As a result, we expend precious resources—time, energy, imagination, political capital—searching (always successfully) for evidence of racism, while our problems grow worse.

Maybe I can make my point clearer by reference to two other minorities. The first group consists of poor whites. There are in American not just individuals but whole pockets of white people whose situation is hardly worse than our own.

And yet these poor whites have their civil rights. They can vote, live where their money permits them to live, eat where their appetites and their pocketbooks dictate, work at jobs for which their skills qualify them. And yet they are in desperate straits. It doesn't seem to occur to us that the full grant and enforcement of our civil rights would leave black Americans in about the same situation that poor white people are now in. That isn't good enough for me.

There is another minority whose situation may be more instructive. I refer to recently arrived Asian-Americans. What is the difference between them and us? Certainly it isn't that they have managed to avoid the effects of racism. Neither the newly arrived Southeast Asians nor the earlier arriving Japanese-Americans, Chinese-Americans, and Korean-Americans are loved by white people. But these groups have spent little of their time and energy proving that white people don't love them.

Opportunity Knocks: Who Answers?

The difference between them and us is in our operating myths. Our myth is that racism accounts for our shortcomings. Their's is that their own efforts can make the difference, no matter what white people think.

They have looked at America as children with their noses pressed to the window of a candy store: If only I could get in there, boy, could I have a good time. And when they get in there, they work and study and save and create businesses and job opportunities for their people.

But we, born inside the candy store, have adopted a myth that leads us to focus only on the maldistribution of the candy. Our myth leads us into becoming a race of consumers, when victories accrue to the producers.

Interestingly enough, this is a fairly recent phenomenon. There was a time when we, like the more recent arrivals in this country, sought only the opportunity to be productive, and we grasped that opportunity under circumstances far worse—in law, at least—than those that obtain now.

Free blacks and former slaves, though denied
many of the rights that we take for granted today,
were entrepreneurial spirits. They were artisans and
inventors, shopkeepers and industrialists, financiers
and bankers. The first female millionaire in America
was Madame C. J. Walker. At least two companies
founded at the turn of the century are now on the
Black Enterprise list of the 100 top black firms in the
country.

Black real estate operatives transformed white
Harlem into a haven for blacks. The early 1900s saw
the founding of a number of all-black towns: Mound
Bayou, Mississippi; Boley, Oklahoma; Nicodemus,
Kansas; and others.

Boley at one time boasted a bank, twenty-five gro-
cery stores, five hotels, seven restaurants, a water-
works, an electricity plant, four cotton gins, three
drug stores, a bottling plant, a laundry, two newspapers, two colleges, a high school, a grade school, four
department stores, a jewelry store, two hardware
stores, two ice cream parlors, a telephone exchange,
five churches, two insurance agencies, two livery sta-
bles, an undertaker, a lumber yard, two photography
studios, and an ice plant [from J. DeSane, *Analogies
and Black History: A Programmed Approach*]. Not bad
for an all-black town of 4,000.

As Robert L. Woodson observed in his book, *On the
Road to Economic Freedom,* "The Harlem and Boley
experiences, which matched aggressive black en-

trepreneurial activity with the self-assertion drive of
the black masses, was multiplied nationwide to the
point that, in 1913, fifty years after Emancipation,
black America had accumulated a personal wealth of
$700 million.

"As special Emancipation Day festivals and parades
were held that year in cities and towns across the
country, blacks could take pride in owning 550,000
homes, 40,000 businesses, 40,000 churches, and
937,000 farms. The literacy rate among blacks
climbed to a phenomenal 70 percent—up from 5 percent in 1863."

Overlearning the Civil Rights Lesson

What has happened since then? A lot of things,
including a good deal of success that we don't talk
much about. But among the things that have happened are two that have created problems for us.
First is the overemphasis on integration, as opposed
to desegregation and increased opportunity. Hundreds of thriving restaurants, hotels, service outlets,
and entertainment centers have gone out of business
because we preferred integration to supporting our
own painstakingly established institutions. Indeed,
aside from black churches and black colleges, little
remains to show for that entrepreneurial spurt of the
early decades of this century.

The other thing that has happened is that we over-learned the lessons of the civil rights movement. That movement, brilliantly conceived and courageously executed, marked a proud moment in our history. The upshot was that black Americans, for the first time in our sojourn here, enjoy the full panoply of our civil rights.

Unfortunately, that period also taught us to see in civil rights terms things that might more properly be addressed in terms of enterprise and exertion rather than in terms of equitable distribution. Even when we speak of business now, our focus is on distribution: on set-asides and affirmative action.

Entrepreneurs and Self-Help

Our 1960s success in making demands on government has led us to the mistaken assumption that government can give us what we need for the next major push toward equality. It has produced in us what Charles Tate of the Booker T. Washington Foundation recently described as a virtual antipathy toward capitalism.

Even middle-class blacks seldom talk to their children about going into business. Instead our emphasis is on a fair distribution of jobs in business created and run by others. We ought to have a fair share of those jobs. But the emphasis, I submit, ought to be finding

ways to get more of us into business and thereby creating for ourselves the jobs we need.

That is especially true with regard to the so-called
black underclass, who tend to reside in areas abandoned by white businesses.

In addition to figuring out ways of getting our unemployed to jobs that already exist, we need to look
for ways to encourage blacks in those abandoned
neighborhoods to create enterprises of their own.
What I have in mind are not merely the shops and
Mom & Pop stores that we still patronize (but whose
owners are far likelier to be Vietnamese or Koreans
than blacks), but also an entrepreneurial approach
to our social problems.

I am not suggesting that government has no role
in attacking these problems. It has a major role. What
I am suggesting is that we need to explore ways of
creating government-backed programs that instead
of merely making our problems more bearable go in
the direction of solving those problems. We are for-
ever talking about the lack of day care as an impedi-
ment to work for welfare families. But why aren't we
lobbying for legislation that would relax some of the
anti-entrepreneurial rules and permit some of the
money now spent on public welfare to be used to
establish child-care centers run by the neighbors of
those who need the care? Why aren't we looking for
ways to use the funds that are already being ex-

pended to create small jitney services to transport job-seekers to distant jobs?

Success Is the Goal

I said at the beginning that I am not a theoretician, but I do have one little theory that may have some relevance to our subject. It is this: When people believe that their problems can be solved, they tend to get busy solving them—partly because it is the natural thing to do and partly because they would like to have the credit. When people believe that their problems are beyond solution, they tend to position themselves so as to avoid blame for their nonsolution.

Now none of the black leadership will tell you that they think the problems we face are beyond solution. To do so would be to forfeit their leadership positions. But their behavior, if my theory is correct, suggests their pessimism.

Let me offer an example of what I am talking about. Take the woeful inadequacy of education in the predominantly black central cities. Does the black leadership see the ascendancy of black teachers and school administrators and the rise of black politicians to positions of local leadership as assets to be used in improving those dreadful schools? Rarely. What you are more likely to hear are charges of white abandonment, white resistance to integration, white conspiracies to isolate black children even when the schools are officially desegregated. In short, white people are responsible for the problem.

But if the youngsters manage to survive those awful school systems and make their way to historically black colleges—that is, if the children begin to show signs that they are going to make it—these same leaders sing a different song. Give our black colleges a fair share of public resources, they say, and we who know and love our children will educate them.

The difference, I submit, is that they believe many of our high school students won't succeed, and they conspire to avoid the blame for their failure. But they believe that most of our college youngsters will make it, and they want to be in position to claim credit for their success.

I suspect something like that is happening in terms of our economic well-being. Many of us are succeeding, in an astonishing range of fields, and the leadership does not hesitate to point out—with perfect justification—that our success is attributable to the glorious civil rights movement: that black exertion and courage made our success possible.

But many of us aren't succeeding. Teenage pregnancy, dope trafficking, lawlessness, and lack of ambition make us doubt that they ever will succeed. But how often do our leaders suggest that the reasons have to do with the inadequacy of the civil rights movement, or with any lack of exertion and courage on the part of the leadership? No. When we see failure among our people, and have reason to believe that the failure is permanent, our recourse is to our mainstay myth: Racism is the culprit.

In terms of the theme of this book, we credit black pride for our successes and blame prejudice for our shortfalls.

I leave it to the other contributors—the experts—to suggest the specifics by which we will move to increase the economic success of black America.

I will tell you only that I believe it can be done—not only because it is being done by an encouraging number of us, but also because it has been done by earlier generations who struggled under circumstances of discrimination, deprivation, and hostility far worse than anything we now face.

My simple suggestion is that we stop using the plight of the black underclass as a scourge for beating up on white racists and examine both the black community and the American system for clues to how we can transform ourselves from consumers to producers.

I used to play a little game in which I would concede to members of the black leadership the validity of the racism explanation. "Let's say you're exactly right, that racism is the overriding reason for our situation, and that an all-out attack on racism is our most pressing priority," I'd tell them.

"Now let us suppose that we eventually win the fight against racism and put ourselves in the position now occupied by poor whites. What would you urge that we do next?

"Pool our resources? Establish and support black businesses? Insist that our children take advantage of the opportunities that a society free of racism would offer? What should be our next step?

"Well, just for the hell of it, why don't we pretend that the racist dragon has been slain already—and take that next step right now?"

The Ludwig von Mises Distinguished Lectures in Economics

Ludwig von Mises (1881–1973) was one of this century's most prominent champions of human freedom. His long career as a scholar, teacher, and author was dedicated to defending private property, the importance of the individual, and limited government. His theoretical work conclusively proved that a free society cannot exist without a free economy.

Each year Hillsdale College presents a series of six or more distinguished lecturers on current economic themes. It is appropriate that this series takes place at Hillsdale College for Dr. von Mises bequeathed his entire personal library of over 5,000 volumes, pamphlets, and papers to Hillsdale. It is now housed in a special section of the Mossey Learning Resources Center.

These presentations are given permanence and a wider audience through their publication as volumes in the *Champions of Freedom* book series. For more information, contact the Hillsdale College Press, Hillsdale, Michigan 49242; (517) 439-1524.

1973–1974
Henry Hazlitt—"The Return to Sound Money"
Benjamin A. Rogge—"Will Capitalism Survive?"
Leonard Read—"The Miracle of the Market"
Israel M. Kirzner—"Capital, Competition, and Capitalism"
Sylvester Petro—"Labor Unions in a Free Society"
Robert M. Bleiberg—"Wage and Price Controls"

1974–1975
John Davenport—"The Market and Human Values"
Arthur Shenfield—"Must We Abolish the State?"
John Exter—"Money in Today's World"
Bertel M. Sparks—"Retreat from Contract to Status"
R. Heath Larry—"Renaissance Man and Post-Renaissance Management"
Robert M. Bleiberg—"Government and Business"

1975–1976
Esmond Wright—"Life, Liberty and the Pursuit of Excellence"
M. Stanton Evans—"The Liberal Twilight"
Benjamin A. Rogge—"Adam Smith: 1776–1976"
Gottfried Dietze—"Hayek's Concept of the Rule of Law"
Anthony G. A. Fisher—"Must History Repeat Itself?"
Shirley R. Letwin—"The Morality of the Free Man"

1976–1977

Rhodes Boyson—"Paternalism: The Good Man's Evil Enemy of Liberty?"

Leonard Read—"The Something-for-Nothing Syndrome"

Philip M. Crane—"$165 Billion in Red Ink: The Eye of the Hurricane"

Anthony H. Harrigan—"Economics and the Future of the Nation"

Henry Hazlitt—"How Inflation Demoralizes"

Roger A. Freeman—"The Growth of American Government"

1977–1978

Earl L. Butz—"The American Food Machine and Private Entrepreneurship"

F. A. Hayek—"Coping with Ignorance"

Ronald Reagan—"Whatever Happened to Free Enterprise?"

W. Philip Gramm—"The Energy Crisis in Perspective"

Jack Kemp—"The Political Relevance of Ludwig von Mises"

Roger Lea MacBride—"The Politics of Ideas"

1978–1979

Dan Quayle—"Von Mises Looks at Congress"

William E. Simon—"Inflation: Made and Manufactured in Washington, D.C."

George Bush—"Is America a Pushover?"

Benjamin A. Rogge—"The Myth of Monopoly"

Alan Reynolds—"Can Government Stabilize the Economy?"

1979–1980

M. Stanton Evans—"Conservatism and Freedom"

Thomas Sowell—"Knowledge and Decisions"

Arthur Shenfield—"Big Government, Big Labor, and Big Business: Parallels True and False"

Arthur B. Laffer—"Would a Federal Tax Cut Be Inflationary?"

Christian Watrin—"A Critique of Macroeconomic Planning from a Misesian-Hayekian Viewpoint"

Walter Williams—"The Poor as First Victims of the Welfare State"

1980–1981

George Gilder—"The Moral Sources of Capitalism"

Antonio Martino—"Statism at Work: The Italian Case; Its Relation to the U.S."

Paul Craig Roberts—"America's Self-Denunciatory Ethic and the Problem of Restoration"

Jay Van Andel—"Economic and Social Challenges of the Eighties"

William Rusher—"Media and the First Amendment"

1981–1982

Israel Kirzner—"Mises and the Renaissance of Austrian Economics"

Fritz Machlup—"Ludwig von Mises: A Scholar Who Would Not Compromise"

Roger W. Jepsen—"Reagan, Stockman, and Supply-Side Economics"

Tom Bethell—"Austrians vs. Supply-Siders"

Frank E. Fortkamp—"Liberty for Schools, Schools for Liberty"

Jude Wanniski—"Inflation, Deflation, and the Golden Constant"

1982–1983

Bruce R. Bartlett—"The Role of Economic Theory in Economic Policy: Supply Side Economics"

Arthur Shenfield—"A Durable Free Society: Utopian Dream or Realistic Goal?"

Lewis Lehrman—"Economic Monetary Reform: Putting America Back to Work"

Martin Anderson—"The National Economic Policy: Prospects for Reaganomics"

Murray L. Weidenbaum—"The Need for Free Trade"

1983–1984: The International Economic Order

David Laidler—"The 'Monetary Approach' and the International Monetary System"

Leland B. Yeager—"America and a Healthy World Monetary Order"

Melvyn Krauss—"Is Reagan Losing the Battle of Ideas in the Third World?"

Kurt Leube—"Denationalization of Money"

Anthony Harrigan—"International Trade: Is There Such a Thing?"

1984–1985: Antitrust in a Free Society

Frederick M. Scherer—"Antitrust: Past and Present"

Dominick T. Armentano—"Antitrust Policy in a Free Society"

Joseph D. Reed—"A National Priority: Public Policy for the Information Age"

Dave Button—"Public Policy and Oil Industry Mergers"

Yale Brozen—"Merger Mania: Social Disease or Healthy Adaptation?"

1986: The Federal Budget: The Economic, Political, and Moral Implications for a Free Society

James M. Buchanan—"The Deficit and our Obligation to Future Generations"

Thomas J. DiLorenzo—"Destroying Democracy: How Government Funds Partisan Politics"

Catherine England—"Debt Financing and the Banking Community"

Melvyn Krauss—"The Presumed International Implications of the Federal Deficit"

Paul McCracken—"The Meaning of the Budget in the American Political Process"
Martha Seger—"The Federal Reserve and the Budget Dilemma"
Richard Wagner—"Constitutional Remedies for Democratic Budget Tragedies"

1987: The Privatization Revolution
Allan Carlson—"From Matriarchal State to Private Family: The Privatization of Social Policy"
Arthur Shenfield—"Privatization in the Socialist Camp: Problems and Prospects"
Dick Armey—"Privatization: The Road Away from Serfdom"
J. Peter Grace—"The Problem of Big Government"
John C. Goodman—"The Privatization Solution"
Stuart Butler—"The Political Dynamics of Privatization"
George Marotta—"The World Stock Market and Privatization"

1988: The Politics of Hunger
Eric Brodin—"Man-Made Famine Throughout History"
Mark Huber—"Private-Public Partnerships and African Agricultural Failures
Robert Kaplan—"Putting the Famine in Perspective"
Mickey Leland—"Is There Really Hunger in America?"

Darrow L. Miller—"The Development Ethic"
Frank Vorhies—"The Black Market for Farming in Southern Africa"

1989: The Free Market and the Black Community
Paul L. Pryde, Jr.—"How the Black Community Can Invest in its Own Future"
Walter E. Williams—"How Much Can Discrimination Explain?"
Charles Murray—"Making Good on a 200-year-old Promise: Blacks and the Pursuit of Happiness"
Willie D. Davis—"Positioning for Excellence in a Color-Blind Market"
Steve Mariotti—"Generating Entrepreneurial Activity in the Inner Cities: Hope for the Future"
William Raspberry—"A Journalist's View of Black Economics"